SHARK-PHOBIA

GRACE NORWICH

SCHOLASTIC INC.
NEW YORK • TORONTO • LONDON • AUCKLAND
SYDNEY • MEXICO CITY • NEW DELHI • HONG KONG

Photo credits: front cover background, page 1 background, page 3 inset, pages 14–15 background, pages 36–37 background, & pages 44–45 background: Peshkov Daniil/Shutterstock; front cover left & page 1 left: Denis Scott/Corbis; front cover right & page 1 right: Leah-Anne Thompson/Shutterstock; page 2 background & page 48 background: KPT Photos; page 3 left: Manda Nicholls/Shutterstock; pages 4–5: Willyam Bradberry/Shutterstock; pages 6–7 background, page 10 background, page 21 background, page 22 background, page 25, & pages 42–43 background: PBorowka/Shutterstock; pages 6–7: ArchMan/Shutterstock; page 6 top inset: rorem/Shutterstock; page 6 center inset: Sebastian Kaulitzki/Shutterstock; page 6 bottom inset: wong yu liang/Shutterstock; pages 8–9 background: Wiltshireyeoman/Shutterstock; pages 8–9: Linda Bucklin/Shutterstock; page 9 inset: James D. Watt/SeaPics; pages 10–11: Doug Perrine/SeaPics; page 10 inset: Rigucci/Shutterstock; page 11 inset: Joshua Singe/Getty Images; page 12: Adam Greg/Newspix/Getty Images; page 13: Fergus Kennedy/JAI/Corbis; page 13 inset: Doug Perrine/SeaPics; pages 14–15: Jeff Rotman/SeaPics; page 15 left inset: Doug Perrine/SeaPics; page 15 right inset: stockpix4u/Shutterstock; page 16: uwimages/iStock; page 17: Willyam Bradberry/Shutterstock; page 18: Doug Perrine/SeaPics; page 19: Galushko Sergey/Shutterstock; page 19 left inset: Jeff Rotman/SeaPics; page 19 right inset: SeaPics; pages 20–21: R. Gino Santa Maria/Shutterstock; page 20 inset: Andre Seale/SeaPics; pages 22–23: Will Schubert/SeaPics; page 22 inset: David Kearnes/SeaPics; page 23: Clover/Shutterstock; page 23 left inset: Masa Ushioda/SeaPics; page 23 right inset: A Cotton Photo/Shutterstock; pages 24–25: Fiona Ayerst/Getty Images; page 25 left inset: Alperium/Shutterstock; page 25 right inset: Soundsnaps/Shutterstock; page 26: Sergey Popov V/Shutterstock; page 26 top inset: BW Folsom/Shutterstock; page 26 bottom inset: A Cotton Photo/Shutterstock; page 27: Willyam Bradberry/Shutterstock; page 27 inset: Larry Gatz/Getty Images; pages 28–29: Ian Scott/Shutterstock; page 29: Lorenzo Mondo/Shutterstock; page 29 left inset: Visuals Unlimited, Inc./Andy Murch/Getty Images; page 29 right inset: W. Poelzer/Peter Arnold/Photolibrary; pages 30–31: Chris Brunskill/ardea.com; page 30 inset: Mike Parry Minden Pictures/Getty Images; pages 31: Helen & Vlad Filatov/Shutterstock; page 31 left inset: Richard Herrmann/Minden Pictures/Getty Images; page 31 center inset: Doug Perrine/SeaPics; page 31 right inset: Visuals Unlimited, Inc./Andy Murch/Getty Images; pages 32–33: Doug Perrin/SeaPics; page 33: ck./Shutterstock; page 33 left inset: David Wrobel/SeaPics; page 33 center inset: Visuals Unlimited, Inc./Andy Murch/Getty Images; page 33 right inset: Doug Perrine/SeaPics; pages 34–35: Suto Norbert Zsolt/Shutterstock; page 34 inset: qldian/iStock; page 35 top inset: Jonathan Bird/SeaPics; page 35 bottom inset: Undersea Discoveries/Shutterstock; pages 36–37: Willyam Bradberry/Shutterstock; page 37 top inset: Julie Lucht/Shutterstock; page 37 center inset: Schmid Christophe/Shutterstock; page 37 bottom inset: Ralf Kiefner/SeaPics; pages 38–39: Catmando/Shutterstock; page 38 top inset: Tom Middleton/Shutterstock; page 38 bottom inset: Jeff Rotman/Getty Images; page 39 inset: Doug Perrine/SeaPics; pages 40–41: Dr. Flash/Shutterstock; page 41 background & pages 46–47 background: PBorowka/Shutterstock; pages 42–43: Dropu/Shutterstock; page 42 inset: Gwen Lowe/SeaPics; page 43 top inset: Gwen Lowe/SeaPics; page 43 bottom inset: Howard Hall/SeaPics.com; pages 44–45: Dropu/Shutterstock; page 44 top inset: Andre Seale/Photolibrary; page 44 bottom inset: David Shen/SeaPics; page 45 top inset: Marty Snyderman/SeaPics; page 45 bottom inset: Marty Snyderman/SeaPics; pages 46–47: tororo reaction/Shutterstock; back cover: Firefly Productions/Corbis

ISBN 978-0-545-31782-5

10 9 8 7 6 5 4 3 2 1   11 12 13 14 15

Printed in the U.S.A.   40

First edition, August 2011
Design by Kay Petronio

CONTENTS

4

Darkness falls over the deep blue sea. A school of colorful fish darts in and out of the coral reef. In the distance, seagulls squawk loudly. All of a sudden, a dark fin breaks the surface of the water. It circles the reef. The fish take cover, sensing the presence of a feared hunter. All is quiet . . . too quiet. Just then, a dark form torpedoes through the water! That can only mean one thing: It must be . . . it's a . . . SHARK!!!

Of all the many creatures in the world's oceans, none seems as scary as the shark. And if you happen to be a small fish or seal or seabird, you have good reason to be afraid of this vicious predator! That's because sharks sit comfortably near the top of the food chain, meaning that while they will eat just about anything, very few things eat them.

It's a different story for us humans. While sharks have been known to attack swimmers and scuba divers on rare occasions, most sharks avoid human contact at all costs. In fact, a person is twice as likely to be struck by lightning as attacked by a shark. So why are so many people terrified of them? The answer has to do with a curious little word: *PHOBIA*.

SELACHO-WHAT?

pho·bia (noun)
"An exaggerated, usually inexplicable and illogical fear of a particular object, class of objects, or situation."

—*Merriam-Webster's Online Dictionary*

In other words, having a phobia means that there is something you're very afraid of, even though there's really no need to be. A lot of people suffer from shark phobia in a big way. Doctors even have a special name for it: *selachophobia*.

Check out this list of other common phobias:

Claustrophobia: the fear of enclosed spaces

Coulrophobia: the fear of clowns

Mikrophobia: the fear of germs

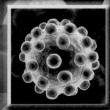

Nyctophobia: the fear of the dark

Tachophobia: the fear of speed

So how do you know if you have **selachophobia**? If you go weak in the knees at the sight of a shark's fin slicing through the water, that's a sure sign. But the truth is, most people would be afraid of that! True selachophobes hate seeing sharks even if they're safe inside a boat or on the opposite side of a thick wall of glass at an aquarium. In extreme cases of selachophobia, people refuse to swim at any beach, even if sharks have never been spotted there. Sometimes they can't even handle the image of a shark in books or on TV. Fortunately, even serious sufferers of shark phobia can get over their fear.

CONQUERING YOUR FEAR

Step one is figuring out why you're so afraid of sharks. Sharks have been made out to be more dangerous than they are, especially in movies and on television. The best example of this is the movie *Jaws*, in which a shark terrorizes a beach town. When the movie first came out, a lot of people stopped going to the beach! Peter Benchley, the author of the novel the movie was based on, later said he never would have written the story had he known what sharks are really like. The best way for you to conquer your fear of sharks is to learn more about them.

SHARKS 101

Let's learn more about what makes a shark a shark. Sharks are cold-blooded fish that have been around for over 200 million years. In comparison, humans have been around for only roughly 150,000 years. During their long existence, sharks have branched off into more than 400 different species. While sharks come in a variety of shapes and sizes, most of them have sleek, torpedo-shaped bodies. When shark-phobes think of a shark, this is what they see.

Let's take a closer look at the shark. Next to each body part you'll find a Fear-o-meter. This will tell you how scary this part is to other shark-phobes.

FEAR-O-METER: HIGH

TEETH

FEAR-O-METER: HIGH

low medium high

By far the worst fear among people with shark phobia is getting bitten while swimming in the ocean. Some sharks have long, pointy teeth, while others have teeth that are shorter and broader. No matter the shape, they can all be used to bite! Despite all the chomping they do, a shark's teeth are pure white in color. However, after the teeth fall out, they may turn brown or gray.

A shark can have up to fifty front teeth and several rows of replacement teeth. If a front tooth falls out, a new one will eventually slide into its place—that way, a shark is always ready to eat! A shark might have more than 20,000 teeth over its lifetime.

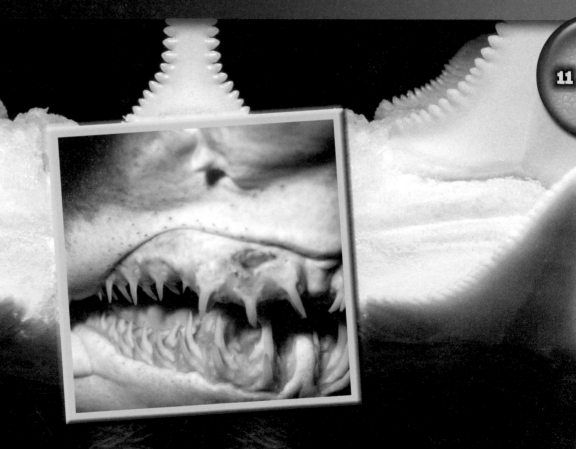

MOUTH

Shark teeth are scary, but so is the mouth that holds them. Especially when it's open wide! On most sharks, the mouth is located on the underside of the head. That might seem like a strange location for biting. But a shark can dislocate its jaw from its skull. That lets the shark open its mouth wide around large prey, including seals and sea lions.

Some sharks eat by taking water into their mouths and filtering out tiny plants and animals with a special body part called a gill raker. These sharks are known as **filter feeders**.

gill raker

EYES

14

FEAR-O-METER: MEDIUM-HIGH

low   medium   high

A shark's eyes work a lot like yours do, except that a shark can see much farther than you can. A shark's eyes are located on either side of its head, instead of being directly in front. This placement helps the shark see all around when it's on the hunt. When sharks bite down on their victims, their eyeballs often roll back to protect themselves from damage.

Even when a shark seems to be sleeping, its eyes can still be open. Scientists think a shark is able to rest one section of its brain at a time. That means it's never really asleep! Pretty scary, huh?

HEAD AND SNOUT

16

Most sharks have long, pointed snouts that help them maneuver quickly in the water. A shark's snout also helps it hunt. Clusters of tiny pores around the shark's head and front end, called ampullae of Lorenzini, detect electrical waves emitted by fish and other sea creatures. The snout is also covered with microscopic taste buds. That's why sharks will sometimes bump potential victims with their snouts—to see if they like the taste. Plus, the snout holds the shark's nostrils, which it uses to sniff out prey.

FRIGHT BITE

A shark has an incredibly strong sense of smell, especially when it comes to blood. Scientists have proved that sharks can pick up the scent of a single drop of blood dissolved in 25 gallons of water!

17

FINS

FEAR-O-METER: MEDIUM

low   medium   high

The sight of a dark fin slicing through the water is enough to give any shark-phobe a serious case of the shakes. That fin is called the dorsal (or back) fin, and it helps the shark keep its balance while it swims. Most sharks also have pectoral (or side) fins that help them move up and down in the water.

FRIGHT BITE

A lot of people like to eat shark. The fin of the shark is considered a delicacy in some countries. Fishermen often keep only the shark's fin, throwing the rest of its body back into the water. This wasteful practice has dramatically reduced the number of sharks swimming in the world's waters today.

BODY

FEAR-O-METER: MEDIUM

The bodies of most sharks are shaped like torpedoes. Some are less than a foot long, while others grow to more than 50 feet! Sharks don't have bones. Instead, their skeletons are made of cartilage, the same stuff your nose and ears are made of. This makes them very flexible.

FRIGHT BITE

Each shark has a line-shaped system of sensory organs that runs down both sides of its body. This is called the lateral line, and it can sense even the slightest changes in water currents. This sense helps the shark detect the movement of prey in water.

SKIN

22

Shark-phobes often expect a shark's skin to be slimy. But in fact a shark's skin is as rough as sandpaper. That's because it is covered with tiny, toothlike scales called dermal denticles. These protect the shark, and they also help it swim more smoothly through the water.

Many sharks have dark skin on their backs and light skin on their bellies. This feature is called **countershading**, and it makes these sharks harder to see in water. Sharks that live in deep, murky waters tend to be brown, gray, or black for this same reason.

23

TAIL

low   medium   high

A shark swims by moving its tail, which includes several fins, from side to side. The caudal fin—the fin at the end of the tail—consists of an upper and a lower section, known as lobes. On some species the lobes are about the same size, while on others the upper lobe is much longer than the lower lobe.

24

Sharks use their tails to warn other creatures, including fellow sharks, not to mess with them. When all is quiet, the shark's tail is straight. But if the shark feels threatened in any way, it will adopt a "threat posture" by curving its tail to one side.

SHARKS BY THE NUMBERS

20,000 total number of teeth that a shark might have in a lifetime

12,000 depth (in feet) at which some sharks live

10,000 distance (in miles) that some sharks roam each year looking for food

2,000 gallons of water that a whale shark can filter for food every hour

100 number of years that some sharks can live

60 maximum number of pups, or babies, that sharks can birth in one litter

50 length (in feet) of the longest shark

WHERE TO FIND SHARKS

Fortunately for shark-phobes, sharks haven't yet figured out a way to live on land. But they have adapted to most underwater conditions, or habitats. Considering that more than two-thirds of Earth's surface is covered in water, that means sharks have a pretty huge hunting ground. Some sharks are lone hunters. Others swim around in schools of up to 100 other sharks. That's a pretty terrifying sight, especially to a smaller fish!

Scientists who study sharks sometimes group them according to the temperature of the water the sharks live in. Here are their three main habitats.

WARM WATER

Many sharks live in this habitat because they prefer water that stays above 70 degrees Fahrenheit. That's why tropical oceans around Earth's equator are often filled with sharks. These sharks are comfortable in shallow waters, so they often cruise close to land.

COMMON WARM-WATER SHARKS

lemon shark

hammerhead shark

TEMPERATE WATER

The sharks that live in this habitat like water between 50 and 70 degrees Fahrenheit. These temperatures are found in most waters of the world. Many temperate-water sharks will venture far from the **coastline** out into the middle of the open ocean.

great white shark

COMMON TEMPERATE-WATER SHARKS

basking shark

mako shark

blue shark

COLD WATER

Sharks that prefer this habitat are comfortable in water that's below 50 degrees Fahrenheit. These sharks are often found in deep waters. Some hang out a mile beneath the surface! Cold-water sharks are often sluggish hunters. The spiny dogfish eats food—such as crabs, sea worms, or plants—off the ocean floor, a practice known as **bottom-feeding**. But others, like the porbeagle shark, can attack fast-swimming fish.

COMMON COLD-WATER SHARKS

Greenland shark

spiny dogfish shark

porbeagle shark

THE WORLD'S MOST DANGEROUS SHARKS

While most species of shark never come anywhere near humans, some can be dangerous. Here are three sharks that you never want to see up close:

BULL SHARK

Where it lives:
The coasts of North and South America, as well as Africa, Australia, and Asia

Why it's so scary:
The bull shark gets its name from its aggressive behavior. It is also one of the few sharks that can live in freshwater, so it can attack people in rivers and lakes as well as in oceans.

bull shark

great white shark

tiger shark

GREAT WHITE SHARK
Where it lives:
Tropical to cool seas worldwide
Why it's so scary:
Also referred to as "white death" and "the man-eater" (gulp!), the great white shark has made the most recorded attacks on humans.

TIGER SHARK
Where it lives:
Tropical and subtropical seas worldwide, especially off the coast of Australia
Why it's so scary:
The tiger shark has exceptionally sharp teeth, even for a shark, and can swim superfast when chasing prey. Plus, it'll eat practically anything, alive or dead.

HOW TO PROTECT YOURSELF

Shark attacks are extremely uncommon, but they do happen. There have even been some incidents off the coasts of the United States. Here are three ways to stay protected:

1 Do not go swimming alone.

2 Avoid risky locations. There will probably be signs posted where sharks have been spotted or attacks have occurred. But if you're visiting a beach for the first time, it pays to ask a lifeguard or a local resident about shark activity. When in doubt, keep out of the water!

3 Don't go swimming if you're bleeding or have cut yourself recently. Remember, sharks are able to smell even a few drops of blood.

4 Never touch a shark, even if it's small or appears to be injured. And if a shark does approach you, swim quickly but calmly away from the area. Splashing or other sudden movements can alarm the shark and cause it to strike.

SHARKS NO SWIMMING

WHAT GIVES SHARKS THE SHAKES

Sharks are definitely some of the ocean's most feared creatures. But there are occasions when the hunter becomes the hunted. Killer whales, which hunt in packs, have been known to snack on average-size sharks. Sharks also have to watch out for attacks from other sharks.

But the biggest threat of all for sharks is humans. Human activity is responsible for as many as 100 million shark deaths each year. The fishing industry accounts for the majority of those deaths. Besides being sought for their fins, sharks also often get caught in nets that are intended to catch other fish. Additionally, water pollution threatens to make some shark species extinct.

SHARK TEST #1

1. Roughly how many different species of shark exist today?

A) 40
B) 150
C) 400
D) 1,500

2. What is the best way to avoid a shark attack?

A) Don't go swimming if you're bleeding.
B) Stay out of waters where sharks are known to swim.
C) Never touch a shark, even if it looks injured.
D) All of the above

3. Which of these sharks is the most dangerous to humans?

A) Hammerhead shark
B) Great white shark
C) Porbeagle shark
D) Lemon shark

4. According to scientists, for how many hours a day are sharks totally asleep?

A) 0
B) 5
C) 10
D) 15

5. Which of the following poses the biggest danger to sharks?

A) Killer whales
B) Other sharks
C) Humans
D) Dolphins

1.C 2.D 3.B 4.A 5.C

THE WORLD'S MOST UNUSUAL SHARKS

Here are six of the strangest sharks that you will ever find:

FRILLED SHARK

This shark likes to hang in the deepest waters of the Atlantic and Pacific, sometimes almost a mile below the ocean's surface. Maybe that's because it's so strange looking! It's named after the frilly gill slits on the sides of its long, eel-like body. But its wide mouth is pretty distinctive, too, especially since it holds more than 300 razor-sharp teeth.

frilled shark

cookie-cutter shark

basking shark

COOKIE-CUTTER SHARK

Don't let the cute name fool you. The cookie-cutter shark takes small, egg-shaped bites out of its victims. Though it's on the small side, measuring just 1 to 2 feet long, this shark has a pretty fierce reputation. That's because it will snack on almost anything, including dolphins, whales, and even other sharks!

BASKING SHARK

This massive shark is second in size only to the whale shark. Like the whale shark, it is a filter feeder. Its name comes from the fact that it often feeds at the surface of the water, where it appears to be basking in the sun. It's been spotted in oceans all over the world. Basking sharks are very social. They sometimes swim in schools of 100!

GREAT HAMMERHEAD SHARK

This odd-looking creature gets its name from the shape of its head, which resembles a hammer. Odder still is the fact that a hammerhead's eyes are on the far sides of its head. This placement helps the shark have a wider field of vision. There are nine species of hammerhead shark in all, but the great hammerhead is probably the most familiar. It is found in warm waters worldwide, both far offshore and near coastlines.

GOBLIN SHARK

Get this shark some braces! While no sharks are considered pretty, the goblin shark is particularly strange looking. It got its name from the goblinlike creature of Japanese

great hammerhead shark

goblin shark

folklore that it resembles. A long, pointy snout and a mouth full of crooked teeth distinguish the goblin shark. It also has an unusual pink color. Goblin sharks have been found in many parts of the world, including off the coasts of Japan, western Europe, and southern Africa.

LONGNOSE SAW SHARK

Here's another shark that's named after a tool. The sawlike snout is the most distinctive feature of the longnose saw shark, which is found off the coast of Australia. The tooth-covered snout accounts for more than one-quarter of the shark's total body length. The shark uses it to swipe at victims or to dig out prey from the muddy ocean floor.

longnose saw shark

SHARK TEST #2

1. Not all sharks are fierce hunters.

TRUE!

While most sharks eat fish, they don't all hunt their prey with deadly jaws. Filter feeders have wide mouths with filters in them. As the sharks swim through the water, the filters catch tiny plants and animals, called plankton, that are suspended in the seawater. The biggest shark of all, the whale shark, eats this way.

2. More people drown than are attacked by sharks.

TRUE!

In fact, the comparison isn't even close. The likelihood of drowning at sea is 1,000 times greater than the risk of being the victim of a shark attack. Even in Australia, where sharks often come close to popular beaches, drownings outnumber shark attacks by a ratio of 50 to 1.

3. Sharks are never found in freshwater.

FALSE!

Some sharks are able to survive in saltwater and freshwater. The bull shark, for one, has been sighted upstream in many of the world's rivers, including the Amazon River in South America, the Zambezi River in Africa, and the Mississippi River in North America.

4. A shark's skin is slimy.

FALSE!

A shark actually has very rough skin, thanks to the toothlike scales that cover its body. You might think the shark's rough skin would slow it down in the water. But in fact it helps it swim faster, by channeling water around its body.

5. Sharks eat only living things.

FALSE!

A lot of sharks are scavengers, meaning they're happy to snack on fish and other sea creatures that are already dead. That meal might include enormous whales, smaller turtles and birds, and even poisonous sea snakes.

GLOSSARY

Ampulla of Lorenzini: a cluster of pores on a shark's or ray's snout that contains receptors the animal uses to detect electrical waves

Bottom-feeder: a fish that eats plants or animals at the bottom of a body of water

Cartilage: tough, elastic skeletal tissue

Coastline: the line between the land and a body of water

Cold-blooded: having a body temperature that changes with the temperature of the environment

Countershading: a color pattern in which the top of the body is dark and the bottom of the body is light so that the shark is harder to see

Denticle: a tiny, toothlike projection

Equator: an imaginary line that runs around Earth, forming a circle halfway between the North and South poles

Filter feeder: an animal that feeds on tiny plants and animals in seawater by catching them in special filters located in its gills

Habitat: the environment where an animal lives

Lateral line: a system of sensory organs that runs down both sides of a fish's body, used to detect vibrations caused by movement in water

Lobe: a curved or rounded projection on an animal's body

Plankton: the microscopic organisms that float in water in great numbers

Predator: an animal that hunts and eats other animals to survive

Prey: an animal that is hunted by other animals for food

Scavenger: an animal that doesn't hunt for its own food but instead feeds on already-dead creatures

Species: one of the groups into which animals and plants are divided